W9-CHQ-843

# Full Turn

Sarah Blake

Pennywhistle Press

*Malibu & San Francisco*

1989

Cover photograph by Phil Bray
Design/typesetting by Susan Galleymore
Cover design by The Groot Organization, San Francisco

Printed in the United States of America
        by The Watermark Press, San Francisco

ISBN 0-938631-08-X

*For additional copies, address orders to:*  Pennywhistle Press
                                              2637 Hyde Street
                                              San Francisco, CA 94109

# Contents

# Acknowledgments

Thanks to Dorianne Laux for her ear, her eye and her voice.

*for my father*
*T. Whitney Blake, 1930–1979*

# Introduction

In this chapbook, newcomer Sarah Blake explores the sacred territory of the domestic. Love and family. Blood and bones. Blake roots herself in the present and struggles with the ghosts of the past, convincingly adept at being both here and there at once. The series of family poems that open the book are narrative and loose, portraits of mother, father, grandmother. In the second section, beginning with "Peeing," are the love poems, spare and eastern in style, reflecting perhaps the author's growing hope to invent her own path.

One of my favorite poems in the book is "Lobstering" which takes us back to the author's childhood in rural Maine. Here we are treated to a deft sketch of Arthur, a solitary and mysterious figure who digs the quarries and keeps the family's generator fueled. "My mother said/he was the reason/we could turn lights on,/so I knew that Arthur was like God,/maybe even was." Arthur looms in the author's memory as a mythical figure: "Ready in the bow/we watched the ocean pulled by Arthur/hand over hand into the boat." When the child finally speaks to Arthur, asking him about the lobsters "What do they do down there all day?", we half expect him not to answer. Like the child, we hold our breath and listen: "Behind me Arthur's voice/cut the night. /They wait to die, he said. /Like us they wait to die." It is this kind of daily language and elemental wisdom that informs many of Blake's best poems.

Waiting for death is a theme that underlies many of the pieces that follow, but it is *how* we wait for death that most obsesses the author. Blake watches, listens and records, learning that death is not to be waited for or resisted, but honored, a distant bell that reminds us to be open to even the smallest of life's offerings.

Poems like "Aubade" and "A Wife Sees Her Husband Truly For the First Time" are the products of these witnessed offerings, and in them we see the author's desire to count every moment as blessed. The poems, presented here are about nothing less than ordinary life: its traps and binds; its singular moments of unsung tranquility; its patient insistence.

When Blake finally emerges from the weight of grief and comes full turn, it is not with a "loud alarum... or a wailing/eclipse of glory," but with a hushed and unhurried joy.

AUBADE

I wake, make tea
and hold the cup in close.
In my nightgown
barefoot on wood floors,
I watch the wind
lift curtains at my sink.
This is what I wake for—
fresh milk poured
dark bread toasting,
the sound of someone else's radio
across the garden.

Dorianne Laux
Berkeley, CA
August 15, 1989

# FULL TURN

On a ferris wheel outside London,
wet and aching with the press of possibility
the loop of life in our lungs,
I begged you to take me right there
pull me up over the roofs
screaming and down
through the moon's dark blanket.

Across the ocean
my father, hot and sick,
slipped his robe over wet pajamas
went to the bathroom
and died there.

No sign
but the steady click of cars rising
falling from the sky
in the ferris wheel's
full turn.

# LOBSTERING

Arthur's face
had grown from granite.
I knew this,
I'd seen the quarries,
great gaping holes where he had dug
to find his nose and ears and bones.

In the mornings
he hauled gas tanks up the hill
on his back from dock to generator,
the clapboard shed that hummed behind our house.
My mother said
he was the reason
we could turn lights on,
so I knew that Arthur was like God,
maybe even was.

Late afternoons
we turned our faces
from the gabled house,
and followed Arthur down to meet his boat,
then out across still water,
sun skating low along the sea
and took the lobsters
from their rockbed sleep.

Ready in the bow
we watched the ocean pulled by Arthur
hand over hand into the boat.
The plop of trap as it broke water,
the rattling crawl of lobsters
chattering in their nets,
were evening words.

Once
after the stars had broken the sky,
I asked about the lobsters
What do they do down there all day?
Behind me Arthur's voice
cut the night.
They wait to die, he said.
Like us they wait to die.

# THE MORNING WORK

That morning Georgie and I
kneeled on the dock
gutting dogfish, the ocean's trash.
Clean slice like a smile
from chin to gray groin,
guts and blue blue membrane
slid out like birth.

And it was birth—
four shiny babies.
Alive they were, alive
had lived through
our happy slicing,
the morning's work.

We took them seriously—
filled a pail with salt water
lifted each tender fish
into the metal womb,
stood and watched
our newborn orphans,
these gifts from a deeper place,

blood of their mother
on the soles of our sneakers.

# LEG LIFTS

Her last summer, my grandmother
did leg lifts from the middle of the four poster bed
whose mattress sagged like a stomach.
Her hands, twisted one step to the left,
were a quiet shrug on her lap,
a soft shoe step away from time.
In her slip, one strap slid
to the up and down of her knees bending.

From a chair under her window
I watched the steady pull of death's sheet
across her hair, wanted
to reach and put my hands
under her legs, push them up
so that my limbs worked for hers,
settling my blood in her veins.

Instead I listened
to her mouth moving in time
to lifts and bends, heard the sigh
of history escaping with her breaths.
Between her shifting legs my family grew
as vines on spring seize new territory
on brick and stone, with every lift
another name given blood and bone
until I knew
whose hands were under whose
pushing up and pushing up,
whose blood had settled
into whose.

# SHE BUILT THE WALLS

Days
she built the walls,
red brick
on another
bloody brick
nails chipped
lovingly
gave away their surface
to the service
of cement
slapped between each block,
scraped and molded
fit to blend
with the way
of the wall.

Nights
she nursed her hands,
bathed them,
(poor fingers,
poor dear tired soldiers)
held them
under water
until umbered grime
smeared the bowl.
Pulled them up
examined every wound,
mourned
her new flesh torn
and ripped,
then swathed them
cleanly, with care.

Mornings
she rose early
took her coffee to the wall,
began again
the steady slap
of mortar, brick
and sand.

# ALCATRAZ

Even the light is gray.
From cells, wrists
dangle gray hands
through cold bars
into the light
into days of wind
beating salted air
in from across the bay.
On New Year's Eve, some say they heard
Tommy Dorsey's band playing,
the grunt and pop
of champagne crowds
across water.

Some days
they heard the slap of wave on rock,
and felt the slap of palm on girls' thighs,
the sighs of movement beneath
their hands pumping red now,
pulsing strong and moving
through block walls,
over roofs, onto ground and out
down cliff, into water, out
and away.

It's so clear this path,
out and through, over and across.
My grandmother,
small and boneless in her bed
sees it too.
In this prison of no making
her hands are gray and folded
waiting as she listens
to her old, black radio
play the song she sang when strolling
in the dark behind her parents' house.

His hands around her waist, she'd turn
her face up to his kiss,
feel his lips along her cheek.
Stars outlined the horizon of his head.

# DAKOTA TERRITORY, 1867

> *"...Something vague and intangible hovering in the*
> *air would not allow her to be wholly at ease; she had*
> *to stop often and look about, or stand erect and*
> *listen...here there was nothing even to hide behind."*
> —Giants in the Earth, O. E. Rolvaag.


Here, she stands alone,
ginghamed back to a blazing sun
one arm up to shield her eyes.
She sees the way of this wide land,
in this clear, blue-skied land
a man on horseback
is the splash of rain on desert roofs.

Here, great chunks of upturned earth
pledge their fruits to the sun.
In the wheat waving
she sees men's dreams growing
on the dead she left behind—
churchbells of Norway, her mother's laugh,
the stiffened weight of the child she buried
somewhere on the trail. Now nights
she tries to hear her sound
above the thud of shovel breaking ground
to bury seed in soil. Dakota, open spaces,
the dream not owned.

# THE ANGLE OF THE LAND

My mother is rebuilding
the stone wall behind the barn.
She wants us all
to chuck a stone in place
each time we pass it by.

I note she is rebuilding
more than just that wall,
she picks up all my words
and puts them where she wills.

The one I don't mind.
It appeals to Yankee pride
to build and shape
and mock the lack of order.
But this other I can't see.
The stones keep shifting, boundaries
sliding to the slipping
angle of the land.

# ATLANTIS

When Atlantis
let go her moorings,
gave all to water
maybe
there was
no loud alarum
no wailing
eclipse of glory,
but
change found
in silent motion,
gentle shiftings,
no push
just
the letting go.

So much of life
descends like this,
like darkness,
quietly.
With nothing more than
shrugs or sighs,
our lives
drift
down.

# I GIVE MY BLOOD

Fall is the right time to die,
air soft, bones breaking down
into dust.  My father knew this,
he slipped into death
as he had into his suits, quietly.
Now his mother waits,
hands clasped and eyes turned
towards her window.
She is already wrapped
in death's comforter.
She watches leaves fall.

These days I hear my father calling
in the slap of line against the masts
on anchored ships. Summer over,
wind moves trees stripped of their sails.

I bite apples hard and sweet,
hold on tight to love in darkness.
I give my blood to the moon each month
knowing I give up children
too red for this fall,
this world of shadows
where rain spills silk
into a still, black pond.

# PEEING

The day I discovered
that I was a girl,
I stood straight as the rest
on that balcony
overlooking Elephant Rock.
And first went Georgie
sending great, high, sweet
streams over and onto
the granite below.
Next Alec, then Timothy
Christopher and Jonathan
braying to discover
the inscriptions they created far below—
a name, figure eights, a circle,
anything they wanted
would appear.

Legs spread, I went after,
aimed and sent my liquid out
and down along my leg.
I watched it pool beneath me
saw that my turn yielded
nothing, would not fly, the day
I discovered that I was a girl.

# AUBADE

I wake, make tea
and hold the cup in close.
In my nightgown
barefoot on wood floors,
I watch the wind
lift curtains at my sink.
This is what I wake for—
fresh milk poured
dark bread toasting,
the sound of someone else's radio
across the garden.

# INTERMEZZO

In a midnight pinball bar
you put your hands on mine
and held them.

I knew then
why the thrush
does not leave its cover
when cornered

but stays to hear
its heart race under seige.

# A WIFE SEES HER HUSBAND TRULY
# FOR THE FIRST TIME

For years
I've watched him now,
seen his hair grow
up and back from his round head,
know the coffee always spills
over his cup
mornings when he pours it after love.
I note his tired eyes
when he comes home at night—
see his shoulders brace
to bear our children high
on top of his head.

But tonight,
between the chopping of the carrots and the thyme
somewhere at the kitchen counter,
I turned to see him standing in the door,
framed by wood—our house,
and thought
so this is him,
thick wrists, warm hands
and heavy limbs that drape me—
like that piece of velvet
I was measuring for the cushions.
It kept falling off the sofa
backwards slowly,
afternoon light caught
in the crushes.

# SHADOWS

In and out
You showed me how to move
without fear that first night,
your white face above me
moved in and out of shadows,
soft sculpture of our coupling
stained in darkness on the walls.

Despite me you are
at every corner
hips forward, head turned.
Tonight, years from our nights,
I am at your table
and caught in your eyes
steady and blue.
You move in and out of my focus
turn and speak to my quiet man
whose hands have held me gently
pulled me in and out of despair
and there you two are laughing
your heads in shadows.
Candles bend and flare,
drop wax beads in hot colors
on the cloth
stretched out between us.

# I DO

She hears
the soft sigh of houses shift,
the give and creak
as floor settles into ceiling -
the song of years moving
through wood and screw -
gently final.
She knows that frames around a window
sag and bend
give way to the weight
of the house -
unless the beams
are married—
wed in wood by nails,
the preacher—Iron—
hammers endurance home
one two one two one two
I do.

# THE GROWING CRY

Your hands
gather me like harvest
pluck my seed from clinging stalk
and move me in for winter—

there in the slow unfolding
bound like root and soil
we start our fingered search
for the earth we two sprang from

and darkness lights your rainfall
slow upon my ground
until I hear the growing cry
of seed returned to soil.

# SHOWER

In the safety of the cold white stall,
among the hot drops flashing
beading in her hair
her fine cheeks brushed back from their bones,
she was a shining body stripped to soul
whose measured voice
she listened to when night fell
and rain railed against her window,
bowed the trees to its wet power
made beggars of the branches.

# WINDOWS

Foghorns
blare the dead home.
Tripping over the night
they lean their hands
into the wind and guide
themselves to me.

I sit, smoke, write
watch them come.
Long hair and nightgowns
wrap their bones.

Palms press the glass
no smudge, no mark, no trace.
The floating faces wait.

Not tonight, I say
not tonight.

# SHEDDING

They had eaten the first lobsters
of the August season. Around the table
fingers dipped the flesh
from soft shells of the shedding fish
into butter steeped in paper cups.

Afterwards she turned off lights,
emptied ashtrays, opened windows
and let the air from the sea
lift her curtains gently
like the laundry on her line
washed and not yet baked
to stiff shapes by the sun.

A moment she watched night
rain darkness on the roofs.
Then began the sliding—
stockings down
dress up over—
to stand forgiven
of her clothes.

She remembered then
the shedders,
the lobsters men most longed for
out on their twilight hauls
for shedders
gave the sweetest meat
shedders
gave the sweetest.

# AUTOPSY OF A POET

What we found was this:
        there were bones in her living room
        stacked, white and polished
        according to body part,
        legs on legs set
        next to toes
        and other digits,
        with, for God's sake, a cat
        curled sleeping
        in the crook
        of someone's arm.

        Neighbors below complained
        she set them dancing
        weeknights around 10
        when, and I quote,
        "the underside of madness
        peeped like lingerie
        from under the hem of a nun's habit."

        That last
        is from her napkins
        (there are thousands)
        wads and shreds
        of words packed tightly
        into the cracks
        that ran the walls.
        Christ, it'll take days
        to figure
        this one out.